RUPERT
AND THE
GRIFFIN

ROBERT HILLMAN
Illustrated by Lance Ross

C.E.

Rupert and the Griffin

Written by Robert Hillman
Illustrated by Lance Ross
Designed by Peter Shaw

Published by Mimosa Publications Pty Ltd
PO Box 779, Hawthorn 3122, Australia
© 1995 Mimosa Publications Pty Ltd
All rights reserved

Literacy 2000 is a Trademark registered in the
United States Patent and Trademark Office.

Distributed in the United States of America by

Rigby
A Division of Reed Elsevier Inc.
500 Coventry Lane
Crystal Lake, IL 60014
800-822-8661

Distributed in Canada by
PRENTICE HALL GINN
1870 Birchmount Road
Scarborough
Ontario M1P 2J7

99 98
10 9 8 7 6 5 4 3
Printed in Hong Kong through Bookbuilders Ltd

ISBN 0 7327 1576 8

1

From his small bedroom, Rupert heard the rooster crow. A little later came the sounds of movement in the village. Two nightwatchmen were heading back to the castle along the cobbled street beneath Rupert's window, their heavy lanterns, swords, and spears clanking, and their minds on breakfast. "Four eggs and muffins," Rupert heard one say. "No – make that five eggs, bacon, and a big slice of toast."

"Another day, just like every other day," thought Rupert gloomily, now listening to the sounds of movement within the cottage. He heard his mother get up, his father, his sister, and … "Any second now," said Rupert, his teeth clenched as he waited for his older brother to come along the passage.

Yes, there it was: the clattering and crashing as Douglas strode past Rupert's door. "Rise and shine, little brother. The world is waiting!" he boomed. Why Douglas had to wear his armor inside the house, and why he always had to boom, Rupert would never know.

Rupert sat up with a sigh. "Time to rise and *not* shine, more like it," he said to himself. Then he kicked off the blankets, pulled on his work clothes, and headed downstairs.

Around the breakfast table, the members of Rupert's family were already busy with their favorite pursuits. His mother had started reading a new detective story; his father was working on a crossword puzzle; his brother Douglas was boasting about his bravery; and his sister, Beatrice, was completing a twenty verse poem for the village minstrels to recite.

"It's called: How Beatrice the Bold Bamboozled the Saucy Sorcerer of the South," said Beatrice, "and it's a masterpiece."

"How delightful," said Rupert, gloomily.

For Rupert had some problems, and two of them were Beatrice and Douglas. They were already very advanced in their bold careers; their names were known throughout the length and breadth of the land. Rupert's name was not even well known throughout the length and breadth of his own home. Well, perhaps that wasn't entirely true – but it felt that way.

"Hey! Baby brother! Fetch my sword and lance!" Douglas would shout.

"Hey you! Dear little fellow, see if you can find my book of anti-wizard spells!" Beatrice would command.

And off they would go to defeat dragons and outwit wizards, arriving home at sundown flushed with success.

Rupert, Rupert who yearned to be known as Rupert the Reckless, what would he do? Exactly what he was going to do today: go to the market to shop for groceries.

"Rupert, the world-famous shopper," he muttered, his basket on his arm.

Once at the market, Rupert knew that he had to face a further ordeal: now he had to listen to songs about the brave exploits and noble deeds of his sister and brother. Yes, the minstrels gathered in the market place every

day without fail, singing songs for a penny. Even though Rupert never paid the penny, somebody else would, and Rupert couldn't help overhearing.

"Here's a new song, a great song, a song you'll all love!" cried one of the minstrels. "Entitled: *The Glorious and Unforgettable Deeds of Douglas the Doomer of Dragons.*" There were ten verses all told, not counting the chorus:

> His arm was strong, his spirit perky,
> He trussed that dragon like a turkey!

If Rupert had wanted to stay around a little longer, he could have listened to his sister's new song as well: all twenty verses, fresh off the press, about How Beatrice the Bold Bamboozled the Saucy Sorcerer of the South. But Rupert headed off for home. He didn't want to drive himself completely crazy.

"Mother, Father," he announced when he reached home, "something has got to change. I'm not going through life known as Rupert the Shopper."

"Is that right, sweetheart?" said his mother. "And what would you like to be known as?"

"Rupert the Reckless," said Rupert.

"That's it!" said Rupert's father, who was bent over a crossword puzzle at the kitchen table. "Eight letter word meaning 'without heed of danger.' Thank you, Rupert!"

"Well, please yourself," said Rupert's mother. "I've faced plenty of danger in my time, and to tell you the truth, I prefer to settle down with a nice detective story these days. Recklessness tends to get a little boring."

"I was very reckless," said Rupert's father, "before I discovered crosswords and chicken farming. Nowadays, I prefer a bit of peace and quiet, a bit of – what's the word?"

"Tranquillity?" Rupert suggested.

"The very word! Tranquillity!"

"Then you won't mind if I borrow your sword and lance?" said Rupert.

"Take them by all means," agreed Rupert's father, "if you can find them. I think they're out in the chicken shed."

So Rupert set off a little after lunchtime with sword and lance, searching for glory. On his head he wore a saucepan for an improvised helmet – the best he could manage at short notice.

The first dragon he encountered eyed him warily.

"I'm not looking for trouble," said the dragon. "Can we keep this peaceful?"

"What on earth do you mean, you're not looking for trouble?" said Rupert. "You're a dragon! You're callous and ruthless! You're supposed to kill me, eat me. Now come on! Make a move!"

"Maybe once," said the dragon, with a sigh. "But there's this guy, Douglas the Doomer of Dragons. If I so much as scorch your trousers, he'll serve me up for Sunday dinner. Sorry, kid."

Rupert marched off, disgusted. He'd try out the sinister wizard who lived in the tower at the heart of the forest.

"And what can I do for you?" the wizard called down from the balcony of his tower. "Are you selling something? Kitchen utensils, maybe? I'm in the market for a new set of pots, as a matter of fact."

"I'm not selling anything!" Rupert shouted back, angrily. "I'm here to overthrow you and break your magic staff!"

"No kidding?" said the wizard. "Look, I'd like to help you, but I've already been done. Beatrice the Bold gave me a very nasty going-over a couple of weeks ago. My staff's in twenty pieces. Are you sure you don't want to sell me that saucepan?"

Things didn't improve during the whole afternoon. Monsters greeted Rupert politely; ogres invited him in for cookies and milk. When Rupert arrived home, he was ready to scream.

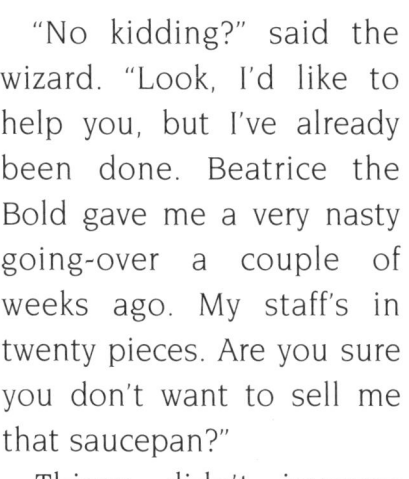

"The whole country has been pacified!" he wailed. "Isn't there a single enemy of the people left?"

"Actually," said Beatrice, with a smirk, "I think I *have* almost cleaned up the place. I'm having a hard time finding worthy opponents myself."

"What about me?" Douglas chuckled. "It's getting so that I have to go fifty miles to find a dragon with any fight in him."

"Of course, there is the Griffin," Rupert's father suggested, secretly winking at the others.

"The Griffin?" said Rupert, suddenly alert.

"Father, really," said Beatrice. "There are some things that we just don't mention."

"Indeed, Father," said Douglas, putting his hand to his mouth to disguise a smile. "Some things are really too horrible even to … ah, even to …"

"Contemplate?" said Rupert, anxious to hear more.

"Yes. Too horrible to contemplate – like what would happen to you if you even went *near* the Griffin. Believe me, baby brother – the Griffin is not for you."

Rupert had to wait until Beatrice and Douglas had gone off to bed before he could question his father again. "Tell me about the Griffin, Father," he said. "This could be my last chance."

"Now, Rupert," said his father. "You heard what Beatrice and Doug had to say. I shouldn't have mentioned it."

Rupert saw that mere pleading would be useless. He tried another strategy. "Are you stuck on the last word of that crossword, Father? I could help you."

"Oh, would you, Rupert? Let's see, eleven letters, starts with R, means unwillingly."

"Simple," said Rupert. "Tell me about the Griffin, and I'll give you the word."

Reluctantly, Rupert's father revealed the mysteries of the Griffin, its terrible history, and where it could be found.

"But do be careful if you approach it!" he said, with a smile. "I'd hate to lose you. Now, what did you say that word was?"

3

The next morning, Rupert rose early. He put on his helmet, took up his sword and lance, and set off to scale the Mountain of Despair in search of the Griffin.

The Mountain of Despair was a very hard mountain to climb. It was steep and rocky and bare as a bone. The wind whistled around Rupert's ears, sounding like the cries of forsaken warriors.

But Rupert never thought of giving up. Fame and glory were waiting for him, maybe just past the next boulder. And whenever he began to feel just a little discouraged, he thought of the songs that would be sung about him, the stories that would be told.

"Rupert the Reckless, that's me. Rupert the Rescuer. Rupert the Ruthless. Rupert the …"

"Ridiculous," said a deep voice.

Rupert froze in his tracks. Who had spoken?

"Show yourself!" he cried, grasping his sword.

"Who says I'm hiding?" said the voice.

Rupert looked up. There, glaring down from the top of the tallest rock on the mountain, sat the Griffin, exactly as Rupert's father had described it. It had the head and wings of a great golden eagle and the powerful body of a giant lion. Its eyes were the color of steel, cool and dark. It was the most magnificent creature Rupert had ever seen – and the most terrifying.

"Defend yourself!" cried Rupert, as he flourished his sword once or twice with some difficulty.

"That's a mighty big sword for a little boy," said the Griffin, and it made a sound which could have been laughter.

Rupert's heart was banging in his chest like a drum. But he stood his ground. "You guard a great treasure," he declared. "I know, because my father told me. I intend to take that treasure. Prepare yourself!"

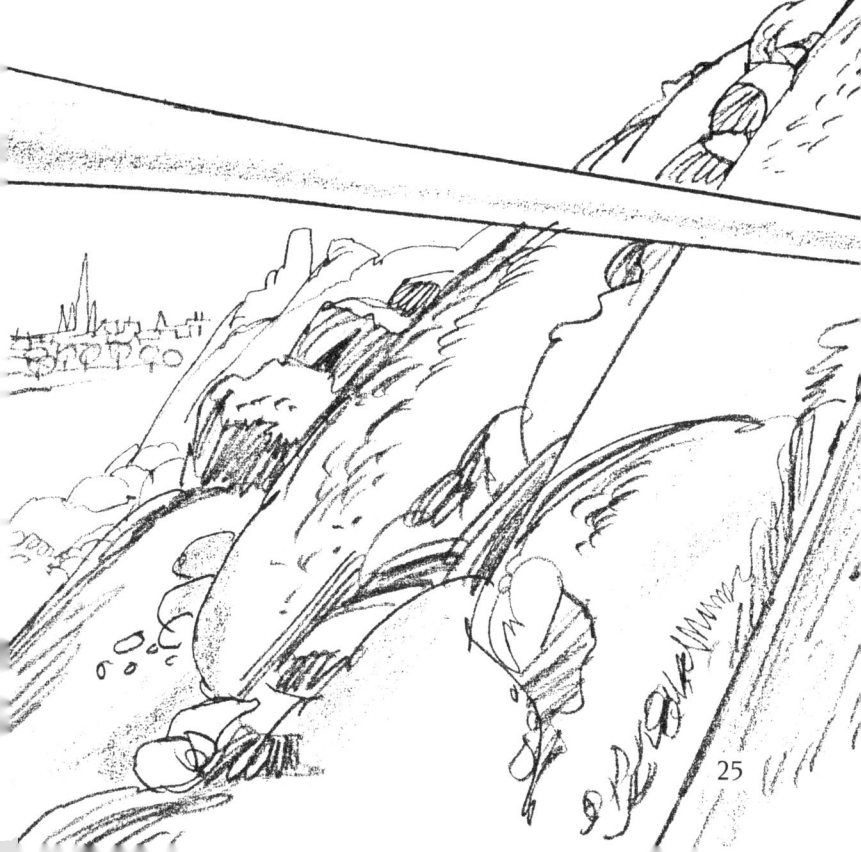

"Sorry to disappoint you," said the Griffin, "but nothing doing. If I didn't guard the treasure, I'd have nothing to do. And I'm already bored as it is."

Rupert was brave, but he was not crazy-brave. The Griffin was twenty times his size. He had no chance. "Then could you at least give me a feather from your head," he asked courteously, "so that people will know that I found you?"

"You know, I might just do that," said the Griffin, and once again it made the sound that could have been laughter. "You're the best entertainment I've had for centuries. A feather's a small price to pay for a little amusement."

And the Griffin reached up with its huge paw, plucked out a single feather, and let it float gently down.

4

Many hours later, Rupert displayed his Griffin feather. "Could have come from a seagull," said Douglas.

"A seagull!" said Rupert. "We're a thousand miles from the sea! No one in this whole kingdom has ever even *seen* a seagull!"

"A pigeon, then," said Douglas. "I'm sorry, baby brother, but I'm not all that impressed."

Bristling with anger, Rupert scaled the Mountain of Despair a second time. He'd had a night's sleep between climbs, but it was an exhausting journey all the same.

"I thought I might see you again," smiled the Griffin from its perch on the rock. "After all, your story was

27

going to be sort of hard to believe: a little guy like you beats a big guy like me."

"You're not wrong," said Rupert. "They didn't believe me! But I know that I can convince them, and I was thinking that … Well, I was wondering if maybe you'd let me have a few hairs from your tail to prove that you really are a Griffin. That is," he added, "if you could spare them."

"A few hairs from my beautiful tail?" said the Griffin. "And you really think that will do it, do you?"

"I'm certain," said Rupert.

"Well, I suppose I can spare you a few hairs. And goodness me, if I didn't give them to you, you'd probably run me through with that lance, right?"

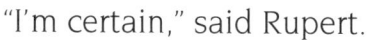

The noise that sounded like laughter followed Rupert a long way down the mountain. He didn't mind. He had the hairs.

"Could have come from the tail of a donkey," said Beatrice, after a glance at the hairs in Rupert's hand.

"They come from the tail of the Griffin!" shouted Rupert. "What would a donkey be doing on the top of the Mountain of Despair?"

"Dear little fellow," said Beatrice, patting Rupert on the head, "I'd like to believe you, I really would. Bring back some treasure next time."

"Mother, Father, make her believe me!" cried Rupert.

Rupert's father, busy with a crossword, looked up and smiled.

Rupert's mother looked guilty. "Sweetheart," she said. "It's just a silly old legend. Your father is pulling your leg. There's no such thing as a Griffin. Why don't you find a nice little dragon, instead?"

"But there *is* a Griffin up on the mountain!" wailed Rupert. "I've seen it! I'll prove it to you, somehow!"

5

Third time up the mountain.

Rupert knew now why it was called the Mountain of Despair. But his rage was so strong that he forgot everything except for the need to prove how bold he had been, how daring.

"Four hours from bottom to top," said the Griffin, when Rupert arrived at the high rock. "That's a personal best, Rupert the Reckless. Well done."

"Thanks," panted Rupert. "I need something else from you, something special."

"My treasure, by any chance?" inquired the Griffin.

"The treasure, exactly," said Rupert. "Then they'd have to believe me!"

"I have to say no this time, Rupert. Sorry, but guarding the treasure – well, that's my job. I told you on your first visit."

"Please!" begged Rupert.

"Rupert, my heart's not made of stone, and I really wish I could help you," the Griffin said sadly. "I mean, I can see your problem, your, um, what-do-you-call-it …?"

"Predicament?" Rupert offered.

"Yes, your predica … Hey! Wait a minute!"

The Griffin disappeared, just like that.

Rupert didn't know what had happened, or why. He only knew that he had failed. He was about to sit down and wail miserably, when the Griffin suddenly returned to its perch on the rock. But the Griffin wasn't sitting still and looking bored, as it usually was. No – it was waving a sheet of paper about wildly!

"Twenty-four across!" roared the Griffin. "A difficult situation. Starts with P, ends with T. 'Predicament!' Rupert, my boy, I've been stuck on that for two thousand years! How about this one? This is a real stumper. Sixteen down. Starts with O, ends with D, fifth letter J. Means very happy. Nine letters."

"Overjoyed," said Rupert, after a moment's thought.

"Overjoyed! Fantastic! Rupert, forget about this 'reckless' thing – just call yourself Rupert the Genius! How do you know all this stuff?"

"My father does crosswords," said Rupert, without much interest.

"Your father does crosswords?"

"Forever," said Rupert.

The Griffin looked flabbergasted. It spread its great wings, flew down from its perch, and picked up Rupert in its paws. "Do you mean to say," it said, "that they have crosswords down there in the little world?"

"That's right," said Rupert. "Why are you so surprised?"

"I got this book from the Sphinx!" bellowed the Griffin. "She told me it was the only one in the world! I gave her ten bags of treasure for it!"

35

"The Sphinx?" said Rupert. "Who's that?"

"A friend of mine – or used to be," said the Griffin, bitterly. "She lives in the desert, and she's very good at riddles of all sorts, the crook."

"And you gave her ten bags of gold for a crossword? That was dumb, if you don't mind my saying so."

"Also a detective story," said the Griffin, "but I finished that ages ago."

"You like detective stories?" asked Rupert.

"Do I like detective stories?" the Griffin thundered. "I love detective stories! I mean, I loved the only one I've read. But there is only one. It's such a pity."

"My mother reads detective stories," said Rupert, beginning to see a solution to his problem. "She's got hundreds of them."

"Hundreds of them? Hundreds? Boy, that sneaky Sphinx!"

"Griffin," said Rupert, softly, "if you fly me home, I'll get you a box of detective stories – and a new crossword. A whole book of crosswords. Fifty crosswords!"

"Fifty crosswords! A whole box of detective stories!" The Griffin was overjoyed. Then suddenly its mood changed. It pushed its huge beak close to Rupert's nose and glared at him out of its great, dark eyes.

"Say," it said, "you're not related to the Sphinx, are you, by any chance? What are you going to want for this?"

"Not even one bag of treasure. Not a penny!" said Rupert. "You fly me home, and the crosswords and detective stories are yours for free."

"Okay," said the Griffin, "it's a deal. But if you turn out to be tricking me, you're birdseed, sonny."

"Please," said Rupert, staring straight back into the Griffin's eyes. "My word is my bond!"

6

What a ride! From his seat in the soft fur between the Griffin's wings, Rupert could see, below, the whole countryside spread out like a picture – rivers, forest, roads, villages. And there was Douglas, threatening a dragon on a hillside fifty miles from home!

"Griffin!" shouted Rupert. "Swoop down over that guy there, the one fighting the dragon!"

"Your humble servant!" said the Griffin, and down it went.

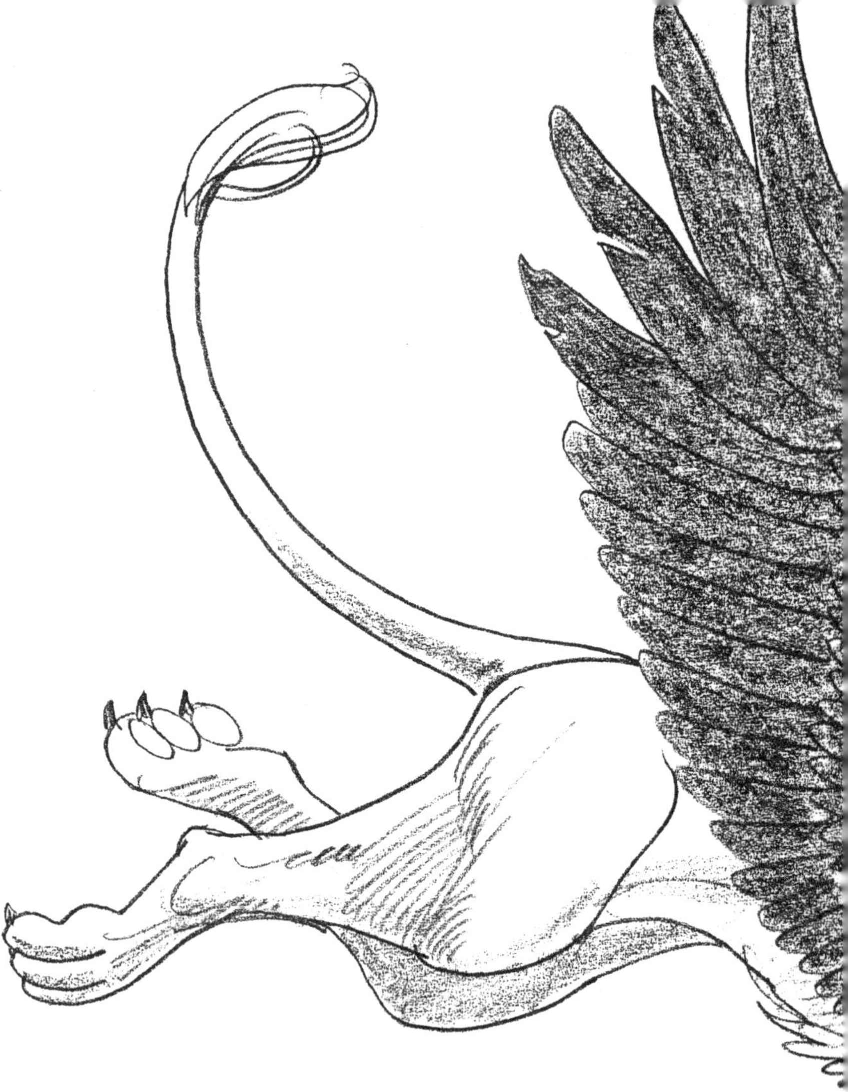

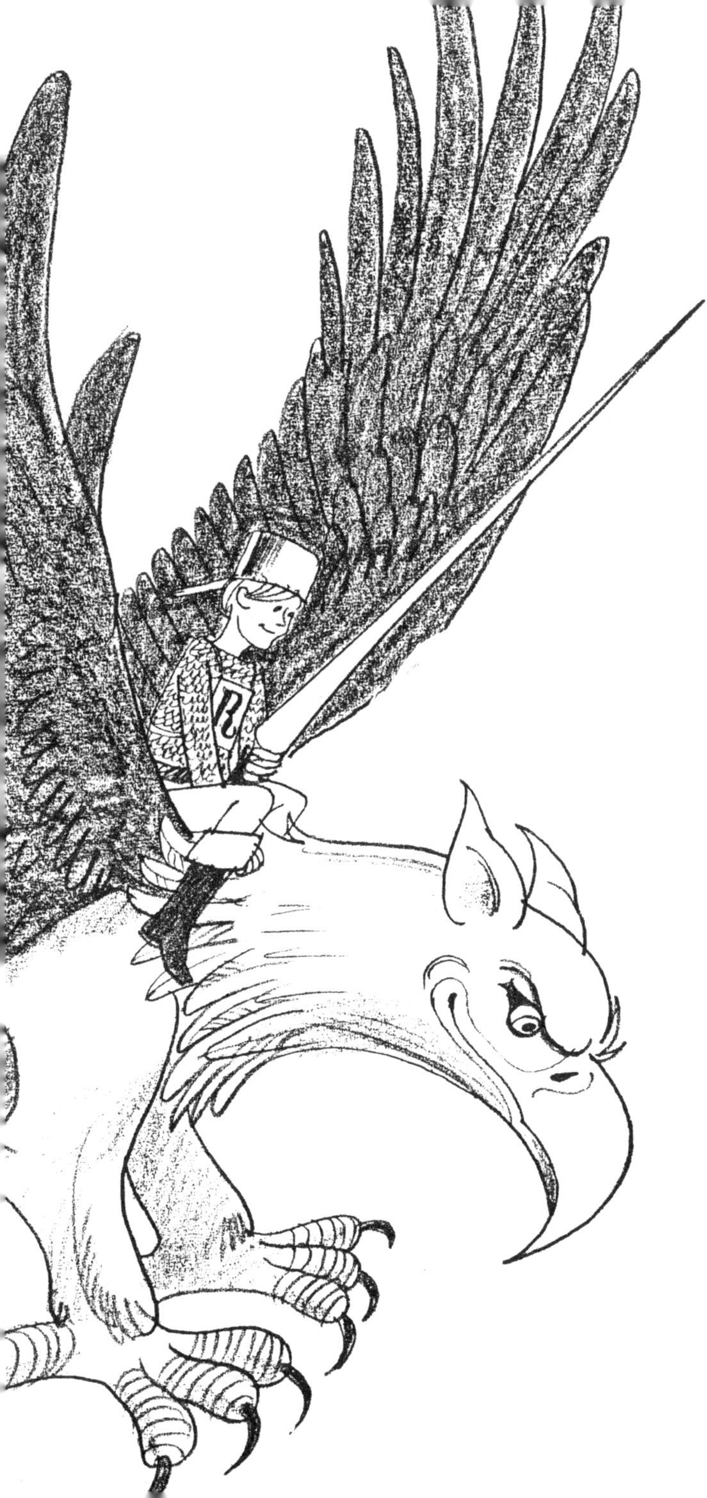

Douglas and the dragon both looked up in terror.

"Hey, Douglas!" Rupert cried out. "Does this look like a pigeon?"

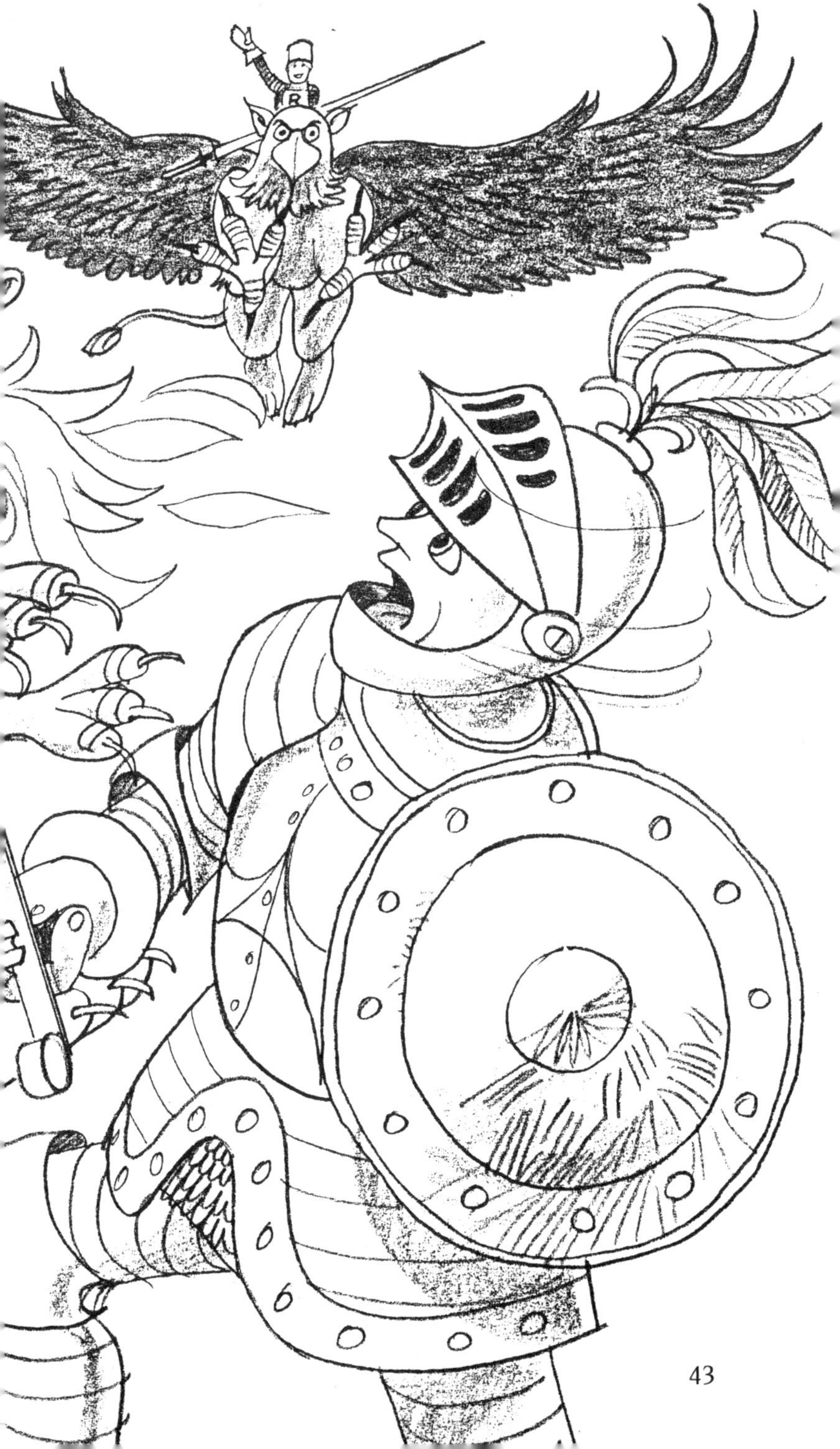

And over there! It was Beatrice, giving a wizard a rough time.

"That's my sister!" said Rupert. "Give her a look at me, Griffin!"

"All included in the fare!" said the Griffin, and it swept over Beatrice and the wizard with a roar like a hurricane.

"Hey, Beatrice!" Rupert called to his sister. "How's this for a donkey?!"

45

Then they were over Rupert's home.

"Griffin," said Rupert, "give me your loudest roar, please!"

The Griffin did just that. It was a roar that shook the windows of the house and made the chickens run for cover. It also made Rupert's mother and father run out into the street, where they saw their son sliding down from the Griffin's back with a huge smile on his face.

47

"Mother, Father," said Rupert, "I'd like you to meet a friend of mine."

The Griffin stayed for dinner: caraway seeds and sirloin. It chatted happily by the fire with Rupert's mother and father, all about crosswords and famous detectives. The Griffin didn't find Douglas and Beatrice all that interesting, however. They had arrived home stunned, and were even more stunned to find the Griffin in their living room with Rupert on its lap.

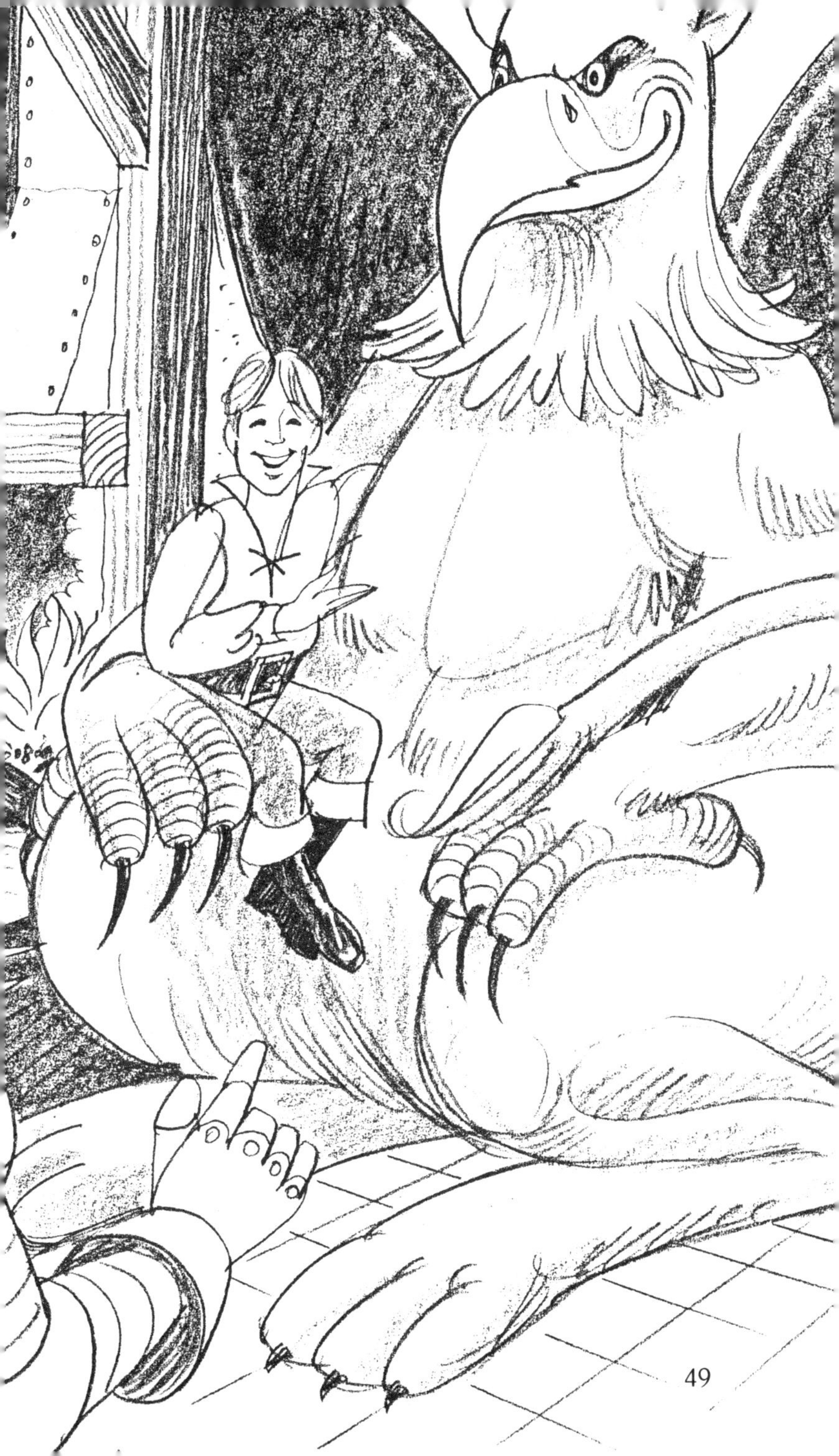

"So, what have you been up to, kids?" it asked with a grin.

'Well," said Douglas, not very confidently, "I skewered a couple of dragons, very big fellows."

"Pah!" laughed the Griffin. "Dragons? They're just kittycats! Leave the poor creatures alone!"

"I completely outsmarted three wizards," said Beatrice, not quite as proudly as usual.

"Wizards?" said the Griffin, and it rolled its eyes. "Wizards are nincompoops!"

"What about Griffins?" Rupert asked happily. "How dangerous are they?"

"Griffins?" said the Griffin. "Rupert, my boy, I can't begin to tell you how dangerous a Griffin is. It even frightens *me* to think about it!"

It was late at night when the Griffin took its leave, a box of detective stories and a book of crosswords clutched in one of its huge paws.

Every person in the village had gathered outside Rupert's home to see the magnificent spectacle. The Griffin waved to them, and then gave a terrific roar that made all the people (except Rupert) fall to their knees in fear and wonder.

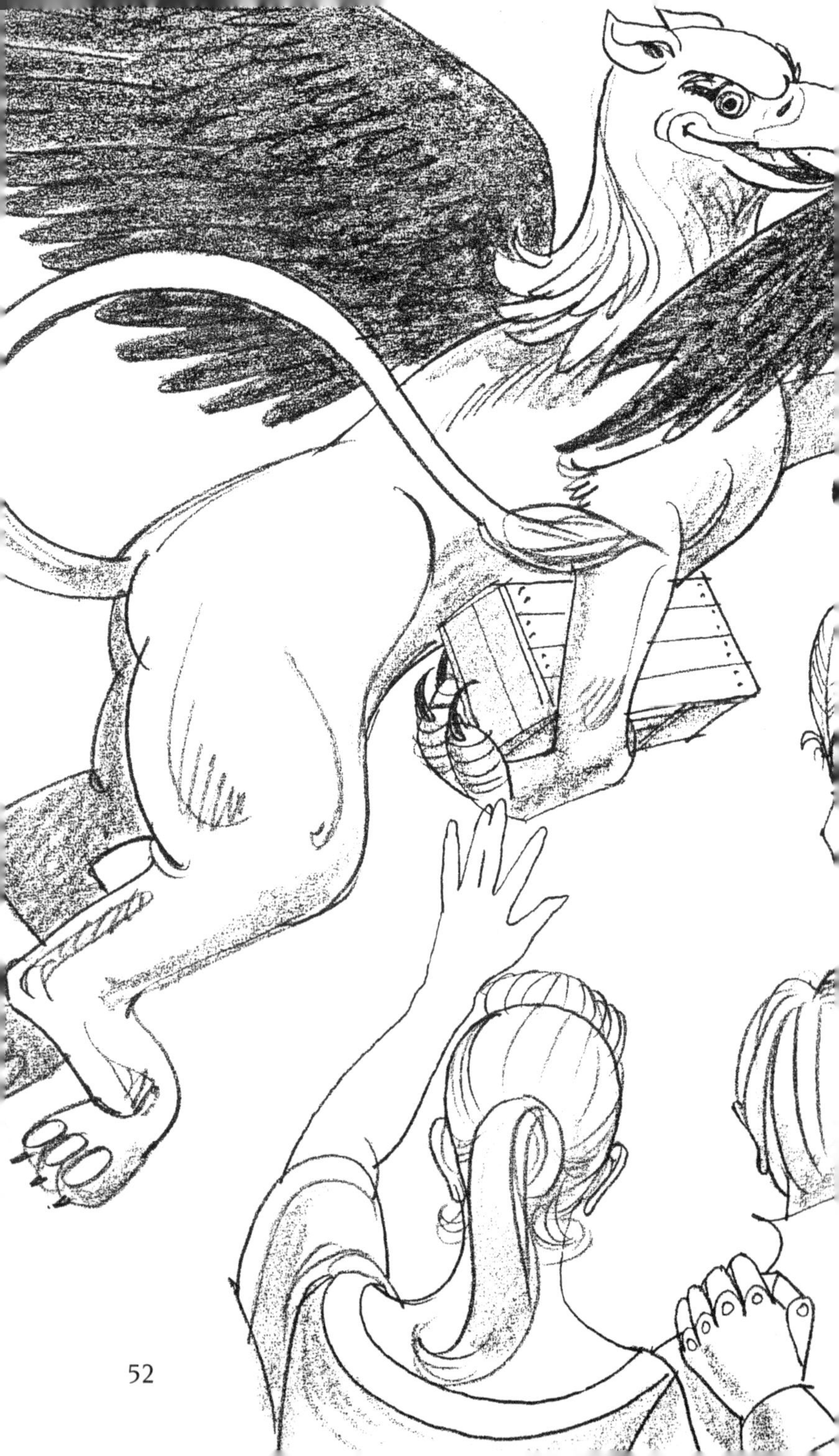

"I have to admit it, Rupert, my boy," said the Griffin quietly. "I'm a show-off!"

It gave Rupert a big hug with both wings, then rose into the air. "Here's a good one for you!" he called down to Rupert. "Four letters, starts with H, means someone who has done a great deed, someone very bold."

"Hero!" Rupert called back, smiling all over his face.

"That's it, son. See you soon!" And off it flew.

Next morning, from his small bedroom, Rupert heard the rooster crow. A little later, the two nightwatchmen passed beneath his window. For once, they were not talking about breakfast – they were talking about Rupert the Reckless and his historic ride on the Griffin.

"Rise and shine," Rupert said to himself as he sprang out of bed. "The world is waiting!"

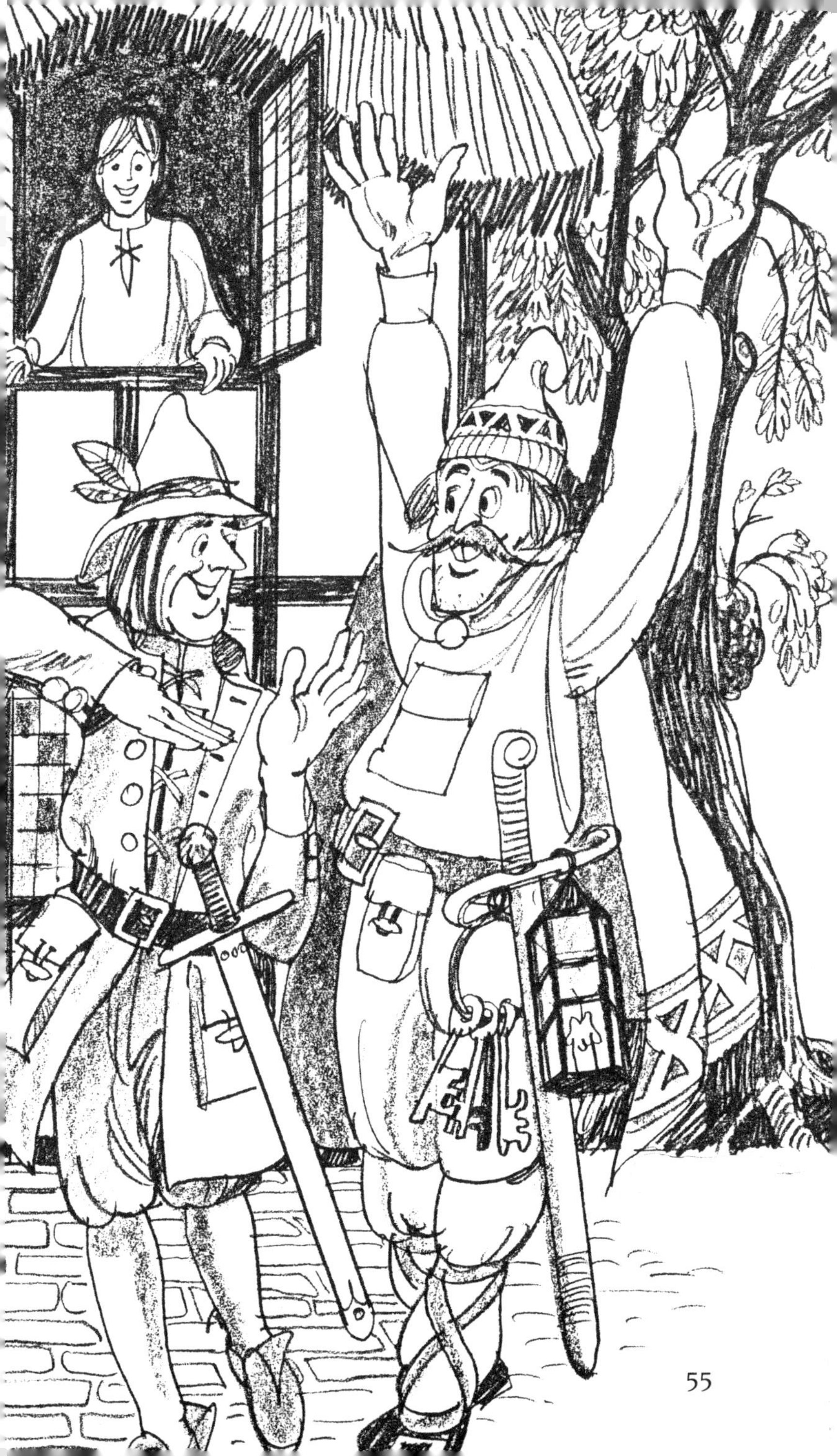

TITLES IN THE SERIES

SET 9A

Television Drama
Time for Sale
The Shady Deal
The Loch Ness Monster Mystery
Secrets of the Desert

SET 9B

To JJ From CC
Pandora's Box
The Birthday Disaster
The Song of the Mantis
Helping the Hoiho

SET 9C

Glumly
Rupert and the Griffin
The Tree, the Trunk, and the Tuba
Errol the Peril
Cassidy's Magic

SET 9D

Barney
Get a Grip, Pip!
Casey's Case
Dear Future
Strange Meetings

SET 10A

A Battle of Words
The Rainbow Solution
Fortune's Friend
Eureka
It's a Frog's Life

SET 10B

The Cat Burglar of Pethaven Drive
The Matchbox
In Search of the Great Bears
Many Happy Returns
Spider Relatives

SET 10C

Horrible Hank
Brian's Brilliant Career
Fernitickles
It's All in Your Mind, James Robert
Wing High, Gooftah

SET 10D

The Week of the Jellyhoppers
Timothy Whuffenpuffen-Whippersnapper
Timedetectors
Ryan's Dog Ringo
The Secret of Kiribu Tapu Lagoon